LINCOLNWOOD PUBLIC LIBRARY

D0998768

Hoot, Moo, Coo

The Sound of OO

By Kara L. Laughlin

2

An owl says hoot.

A cow says moo.

5

6

How about
a kangaroo?

A goose says honk.

9

A dove says coo.

How about a whole zoo?

14

A boat goes toot.

A rocket zooms.

17

18

Listen. Can you hear the moon?

Hoot. Moo. Coo. What does our world say to you?

Word List:

boom	moo
coo	moon
goose	toot
hoot	zoo
kangaroo	zoom

Note to Caregivers and Educators

The books in this series are based on current research, which supports the idea that our brains are pattern-detectors rather than rules-appliers. This means children learn to read easier when they are taught the familiar spelling patterns found in English. As children encounter more complex words, they have greater success in figuring out these words by using the spelling patterns.

Throughout the series, the texts allow the reader to practice and apply knowledge of the sounds in natural language. The books introduce sounds using familiar onsets and *rimes,* or spelling patterns, for reinforcement.

For example, the word *cat* might be used to present the short "a" sound, with the letter *c* being the onset and "_at" being the rime. This approach provides practice and reinforcement of the short "a" sound, as there are many familiar words made with the "_at" rime.

The stories and accompanying photographs in this series are based on time-honored concepts in children's literature: well-written, engaging texts and colorful, high-quality photographs combine to produce books that children want to read again and again.

Dr. Peg Ballard
Minnesota State University, Mankato

The Child's World®
childsworld.com

Published by The Child's World®
1980 Lookout Drive • Mankato, MN 56003-1705
800-599-READ • www.childsworld.com

PHOTO CREDITS

© 977_ReX_977/Shutterstock.com: cover (cow), 5;
Africa Studio/Shutterstock.com: 21; Alexander Sviridov/
Shutterstock.com: 9; Bradley Blackburn/Shutterstock.com:
6; Mariusz Bugno/Shutterstock.com: 14; MyImages-Micha/
Shutterstock.com: 13; Naypong Studio/Shutterstock.com:
10; cover (dove); Phant/Shutterstock.com: cover (owl), 2;
Sergey Nivens/Shutterstock.com: 17; vovan/Shutterstock.
com: 18

Copyright © 2020 by The Child's World®
All rights reserved. No part of this book may be
reproduced or utilized in any form or by any means
without written permission from the publisher.

ISBN 9781503835375
LCCN 2019944782

Printed in the United States of America

ABOUT THE AUTHOR

Kara L. Laughlin is an artist and writer who lives in Virginia with her husband, three kids, two guinea pigs, and a dog. She is the author of two dozen nonfiction books for kids.